Jumpstart Prayers!

Pastor Rachel Blankenship

DEDICATION

I want to say a huge thank you to my children, my family and all of the people in my life who have supported and encouraged me along this journey! I appreciate it more than you know!
Thank you!

Hello friends!

Welcome to your Jumpstart Prayer book! Prayer is so important and such a gift! Our days should begin and end in prayer to our Father! I have put together 30 individual prayers to help jumpstart your mornings in open communication with God! These are prayers to have you focus on who He is and who you are in Him! In addition to the prayers, I have provided note pages for each day. I placed two questions at the top of each page as a point of focus. You may write in your own thoughts or a word that He gives you during your personal prayer time! Enjoy!

~Love and Blessings~

Colossians 4:2
"Devote yourselves to prayer, being watchful and thankful."

1 Chronicles 16:11
"Look to the Lord and his strength; seek his face always."

Dear God,

Thank you for the opportunity to have direct communication with you. You gave us such a gift in being able to have open access to speak to you at any moment that we want. You are always available and willing to come close to us at any point that we reach out. Help us to receive revelation of who you are and what your will is for us.

In Jesus' name I pray, Amen.

Take a moment to listen…. what in your own heart do you want to say?

What is He saying back to you?

"You will pray to him, and he will hear you, and you will fulfill your vows."

Dear Lord,

I am grateful that your love for me is enough to pour out not only blessings on me, even though I am so undeserving, but pour them out in abundance. Guide my understanding, to know that these blessings don't just come from what I can see in the natural, but from an abundance that I cannot even begin to comprehend. Open my heart and mind, Lord, to receive all the blessings that you have for me. Let me be mindful to recognize every time you show up and give you the glory through it all.

In Jesus' name, Amen.

Take a moment to listen…. what in your own heart do you want to say?

What is He saying back to you?

Romans 12:2
"Do not conform to the pattern of this world, but be transformed by the renewing of your mind. Then you will be able to test and approve what God's will is--his good, pleasing and perfect will."

Dear God,

I appreciate your willingness to lead my heart, for showing me where to go and helping me stay in your perfect will for my life. It is not always easy to stand for my beliefs; it is not always easy to say no to my flesh and yes to the things of you. Thank you for being my continued source of peace and strength no matter what comes my way. Your plans for me are so much greater than I could ever have planned for myself. Remind me to keep my mind focused on the things of you so that I can continue to walk in your will and in your power.

In Jesus' name, Amen.

Take a moment to listen…. what in your own heart do you want to say?

What is He saying back to you?

Psalm 141:2
"May my prayer be set before you like incense; may the lifting up of my hands be like the evening sacrifice."

Dear Heavenly Father,

I want to take time this morning to just praise you for who you are! Allow me to open my heart to you Lord. Help me to remember to always have your praise on my lips, even when it is tough, even when it is a sacrifice, Lord. Because no matter what my present circumstances are, no matter how I may be feeling this morning, you Lord are worthy of my praise. For everything you have done, all you will do and all that you are, you are worthy of continued praise. Thank you, Lord!

In the name of Jesus, I pray, Amen.

Take a moment to listen….what in your own heart do you want to say?

What is He saying back to you?

Jeremiah 29:12
"Then you will call on me and come and pray to me, and I will listen to you"

Dear Lord,

I am so thankful that you love me the way that you do! It is amazing that you loved me enough to take your time to create me by hand. You created me individually and perfectly, to be exactly what you wanted me to be. Then you went a step further to design a propose that only I can carry out and equipped me with everything I need to do it. I am so grateful for your Word. Grateful that it is an unchanging reminder of who YOU say I am. Thank you for loving me so much that no matter what I may do or may encounter, I can always turn to you. In those moments, you quiet my heart with your love and rejoice over me in such an extravagant way. Let me keep my true worth fresh in my mind and let me never forget how important I am to you. Remembering how much I am genuinely and unconditionally loved by you!

In Jesus' name I pray, Amen.

Take a moment to listen....what in your own heart do you want to say?

What is He saying back to you?

Romans 8:26
"In the same way, the Spirit helps us in our weakness. We do not know what we ought to pray for, but the Spirit himself intercedes for us through wordless groans."

Dear God,

Thank you for your perfect will for my life! I appreciate that you have a plan that is better than my own and a plan that never fails! Lead my heart to trust in your plan above my own. Your word says in Jeremiah 29:11, that you have a plan to not harm me, but to give me a hope and a future. Even if I don't understand what you are doing or how you are going to accomplish it, you have a plan. You, Lord, see the bigger picture from beginning to the end. You know exactly how to position me and prepare me for the greatness of your plan. I am thankful that you love me enough to create me to be a part of your plan and that you lead me along your perfect path to accomplish your will.

In Jesus' name, Amen.

Take a moment to listen….what in your own heart do you want to say?

What is He saying back to you?

Romans 12:12
"Be joyful in hope, patient in affliction, faithful in prayer"

Dear Lord,

As I start another day, allow me to be mindful of all the things you are at work in. Open my eyes to see that each thing you have created was done with great love and great purpose. Lead my heart, Lord, to appreciate everything I have and am given. Guide me so that I may not ever take anything for granted, but instead, utilize, honor, and appreciate them the way that you intended. Guard my mind as I go about this day. Keep my mind focused on the things of you and my heart full of your love.

In Jesus' name, Amen.

Take a moment to listen....what in your own heart do you want to say?

What is He saying back to you?

Dear Heavenly Father,

It is such a gift to be your child! I am wonderfully made in my own perfect way and with purpose in me. It is amazing to know that I will be the only one ever created this exact way. Since you took so much care in designing me and defining me, you took equal time in giving me my identity and therefore, the path of my calling can only come from you. I am grateful, Lord, that you have given me your word to remind me of each of those facts. Assist me in remembering my true identity, in a world that did not even accept or understand Jesus. I am called to be set apart. Give me the strength in moments of persecution, Lord, and allow me to understand that it is their own lack of knowledge that leads them to that thinking, not me. Help me remember to only let you and your word be the one that tells me who I am. Give me the courage to continue to live my life devoted to you.

In Jesus' name I pray, Amen.

Take a moment to listen....what in your own heart do you want to say?

What is He saying back to you?

Psalm 145:18
"The Lord is near to all who call on him, to all who call on him in truth."

Dear God,

Your word is a lifeline, a source of wisdom, guidance and so much more. I am so grateful for the ability to have it and live in a time where it is so readily available. Thank you for giving me access to a word that has always been and will always be. You have given me access to an unshakable, unfailing, unending, living word to guide me on my journey through life. Remind me to truly appreciate it as the gift it is and not take it for granted. Lord, you really have crafted your written word in such a magnificent way, that I have a complete blueprint and help for my entire life. There is an answer to everything I could ever need! It can bring fresh perspective and guidance, no matter what I face or how many times I have read it! Encourage me in my heart to slow down enough to read, study and breathe in your precious words

.

In Jesus' name, Amen.

Take a moment to listen....what in your own heart do you want to say?

What is He saying back to you?

1 Thessalonians 5:17
"pray continually"

Dear Lord,

I am so thankful for your faithfulness! Thank you for never failing me! Thank you for loving me enough to chase me down, while reaching out through the darkest moments and giving me your hand. Thank you for being so generous to me. I am grateful that no matter what you ask of me, there will never come a day that I could give more than the blessings you are willing to pour out in my life. I am so thankful for your blessings and your willingness to extend your strength and peace when mine seems to be depleted. I appreciate your unfailing willingness to extend such love and grace even when I am so unworthy, Lord! I love you and thank you for the way you love me!

In Jesus' name I pray, Amen.

Take a moment to listen....what in your own heart do you want to say?

What is He saying back to you?

Dear God,

Let my heart stay in meditation of your goodness and mercy. Give me eyes to see and ears to hear everything you are doing in my life. Help me to see your workmanship in everything. Help me to focus on who you are, what you can do and who you call me to be. Help me to remember that you are big enough to move any mountain, but that you also seek to be as close to me as a best friend. Let me appreciate such an amazing opportunity. Let me realize what a blessing it is to be able to have a close and intimate relationship with the creator of the universe! And therefore, forever sing your praise!

In Jesus' name I pray, Amen.

Take a moment to listen....what in your own heart do you want to say?

What is He saying back to you?

"Call to me and I will answer you and will tell you great and unsearchable things you do not know."

Dear Lord,

You are such a good and loving shepherd! You are so full of love, wisdom, mercy, and knowledge. I am grateful that you love your flock enough to leave the 99 who you know are safe, to find the one who has wandered off. It is such a gift to be able to come into relationship with you and serve you. You truly are everything we could ever need and more. Let me always be mindful of your love and let me extend that same love to those around me.

In the name of Jesus I pray, Amen.

Take a moment to listen....what in your own heart do you want to say?

What is He saying back to you?

Psalm 34:17
"The righteous cry out, and the Lord hears them; he delivers them from all their troubles."

Dear God,

Thank you for the victory that I have in you! Thank you for loving me enough to carry all of my sins to the cross, letting it die with you and taking the very keys to hell so that nothing, not even death, could keep us defeated. Let me remember, Lord, that the battles I face have already been won. Allow me to recognize that I have already been given the victory if I will receive it and walk in it. I am thankful that because of your great love, I don't have to walk around defeated or bound up by fear! Help me to see that it is already done and walk fully in the Godfidence you gave your life to give me!

In Jesus' name, Amen.

Take a moment to listen....what in your own heart do you want to say?

What is He saying back to you?

John 15:16
"You did not choose me, but I chose you and appointed you so that you might go and bear fruit-fruit that will last-and so that whatever you ask in my name the Father will give you."

Dear Lord,

I appreciate the unfailing stability of your kingdom! I am thankful that I have the opportunity to serve you and your kingdom, Lord. Remind my heart to be grateful each day for salvation. It is truly a gift that I have been adopted into your kingdom to be joint heirs with Jesus! Encourage my heart to whole-heartedly offer you all that I have and all that I am in service to you as an act of worship for all that you are and all that you have done for me. You gave it all for me and that is worth me giving my all-in response, as an act of service and gratitude.

In Jesus name I pray, Amen.

Take a moment to listen....what in your own heart do you want to say?

What is He saying back to you?

James 5:16
"Therefore confess your sins to each other and pray for each other so that you may be healed. The prayer of a righteous person is powerful and effective."

Dear Heavenly Father,

I am so honored to have a direct connection with you and that you then created us in such a way that we were meant to be in relationship with one another. Thank you for creating us to help each other and support one another. Help me to remember to be open to those walking alongside me in this life. Remind me to encourage others, share my testimonies of what you have done in my life and to not be afraid to reach out or seek wise counsel when necessary. Allow me to grow in my love for others so that I can connect with them and encourage them to stay strong in this race we are all running together.

In Jesus' name, Amen.

Take a moment to listen....what in your own heart do you want to say?

What is He saying back to you?

Dear Lord,

I come to you today and thank you for being a living God. I am grateful that you are always with me, always teaching me, growing me, and breathing new life into me! Thank you for continuing to have mercy and patience with me as I grow. I appreciate, Lord, that when I stay close to you, you honor my faithfulness to you. I thank you for all the blessings that you continue to pour out on me simply, because you love me. Help my eyes and heart be open to see all the blessings that you give and let my eyes see your hand at work everywhere and in everything.

In Jesus' name I pray, Amen.

Take a moment to listen....what in your own heart do you want to say?

What is He saying back to you?

"If you remain in me and my words remain in you, ask whatever you wish, and it will be done for you."

Dear God,

Your written and living word is such an asset to me! I am glad that it is written in a way that instructs me, guides me, corrects me, loves on me, and gives me hope. It is the one book that can read me as I read it. Guide my heart Lord, to appreciate it for the precious gift that it really is. Place a true hunger for your word within me. Allow my heart to have the desire for the wisdom and revelation it holds. Help me to read it with an open mind of what you would want to reveal to me through it.

In the name of Jesus I pray, Amen.

Take a moment to listen….what in your own heart do you want to say?

What is He saying back to you?

Psalm 55:17
"Evening, morning and noon I cry out in distress,
and he hears my voice."

Dear Lord,

Thank you for your grace. Thank you, Lord, that you never stop extending your grace and mercy to your child. Thank you for your faithfulness to me! I open myself to receive your love, grace and mercy and my heart to rejoice when I see it extended to others. Encourage me to prioritize you in my life. Help me to prioritize my conversations with you, reading your word, and spending time in your house. Let me remember that it is only when I am full of you that I can extend the love, grace, and mercy that you place within me, to those around me.

In Jesus' name I pray, Amen.

Take a moment to listen....what in your own heart do you want to say?

What is He saying back to you?

Dear God,

Thank you for being my strength when I am weak. Thank you for always being my place of refuge and peace that I may turn to at any moment. I am thankful that you know exactly what I always need and that you are there ready and willing to provide me with exactly what I need. I am grateful for the boldness and assurance that you give me; knowing that if I have you by my side, there is nothing I cannot do. Thank you for not only always walking with me, but also for going before me and standing behind me. Allow me to realize how truly "covered" I really am and let that knowledge help me to walk in confidence and not fear.

In Jesus' name I pray, Amen.

Take a moment to listen....what in your own heart do you want to say?

What is He saying back to you?

Romans 8:28
"And we know that in all things God works for the good of those who love him, who have been called according to his purpose."

Dear Heavenly Father,

It is a brand-new day full of opportunity. I come to you and truly thank you for this day. I appreciate you keeping me and covering me to bring me to another day. If I am seeing it, there is a purpose waiting ahead! I appreciate the greatness of your works, the goodness of your will and the steadfastness of your love. Allow me to have eyes that watch with expectancy for you to move in great ways today, and every day! Let my heart always trust in your plans.

In Jesus' name, Amen.

Take a moment to listen....what in your own heart do you want to say?

What is He saying back to you?

Dear God,

Today I am grateful for your light! You knew that we would need your light in this dark world and that others would need to see your light through me. I am grateful that your light is strong enough to destroy all darkness in my life and in the lives of those around me! Open my eyes to recognize and appreciate all the ways you intervene in my life. Let me be mindful so that I do not take a single one of them for granted, but instead truly appreciate them. Be with me, Lord, in the upcoming days and weeks. Allow me to face whatever it may hold, with boldness and willingness to continue to shine your light!

In Jesus' name I pray, Amen.

Take a moment to listen....what in your own heart do you want to say?

What is He saying back to you?

1 Peter 3:12
For the eyes of the Lord are on the righteous
and his ears are attentive to their prayer,
but the face of the Lord is against those who do evil."

Dear Lord,

On this day, I just thank you for your gift of eternal life.
Thank you for the opportunity to be spiritually reborn. Thank
you for the ability to take off the life that we have created,
submit it to you and you transform it into something
completely new! Thank you, Lord, that not only did you go
and prepare a place for me to spend my eternal life, but you
also allow me to walk in blessings and abundance while still
here on Earth! Open my heart, Lord. Place a desire within me
to walk closer and closer with you daily. Let me seek your
vision for me while I am here and begin to align my life with
that vision, so that you can bring me into the fullness of what
you have called me to do.

In the name of Jesus I pray, Amen.

Take a moment to listen....what in your own heart do you want to say?

What is He saying back to you?

Luke 22:31-32
"Simon, Simon, Satan has asked to sift all of you as wheat. But I have prayed for you, Simon, that your faith may not fail. And when you have turned back, strengthen your brothers."

Dear God,

I am so grateful for your willingness to pick me up right where you found me, and never holding it against me. Thank you for continuing to pick up me so lovingly, dust me off and set me back on the right path, anytime that I go wandering away. I appreciate, Lord, that your plan is always restoration and redemption; and if that isn't enough Lord, you take it a step further and give me a future beyond my imagination, if I will just be willing to walk in it. I am not worthy Lord, yet you love me in the most beautiful way in spite of me. I thank you for your will, your plans, your ways, and your love, and I thank you for making me everything that I am! Let me seek to always be a good representation of all that you are.

In Jesus' name, Amen.

Take a moment to listen....what in your own heart do you want to say?

What is He saying back to you?

Psalm 121:1-2

"I lift up my eyes to the mountains— where does my help come from? My help comes from the Lord, the Maker of heaven and earth."

Dear Lord,

Thank you for your peace. I appreciate that no matter what I may go through, if I am willing to get into your word and spend time in your presence, you restore my heart. Lord, your presence here with us is such a blessing. I am so grateful Lord, that just by calling your name, you can trade my chaos for calm, my fears, and storms for peace. You are so amazing! Help me to not just speak or pray about all that you do and how amazing you are, but LIVE it each and every day. Remind me to stay full of you, Lord, because it is when I am full of you Lord, I can be a breathing, walking, powerful testimony of all you are!

In Jesus' name I pray, Amen.

Take a moment to listen....what in your own heart do you want to say?

What is He saying back to you?

James 5:13
"Is anyone among you in trouble? Let them pray. Is anyone happy?
Let them sing songs of praise."

Dear God,

On this day, help me to be mindful to give thanks for all that I have in my life. Allow my heart to turn its focus back to you! For it is only, because of you that I have anything and everything that I have in this life. You, Lord, are my greatest gift and greatest blessing. It is only through you that I can enjoy the true abundance of life. Help me to remember all you do not just today, but every day. Let me reflect on you today and all you have done. Encourage that reflection to grow and strengthen my faith in who you are and who you say I am. Rekindle the fire within me to seek to be only who you call me to be, no matter how loud the world gets, because it is only really your say-so that matters.

In Jesus' name I pray, Amen.

Take a moment to listen....what in your own heart do you want to say?

What is He saying back to you?

Zechariah 13:9
"This third I will put into the fire; I will refine them like silver and test them like gold. They will call on my name and I will answer them;
I will say, 'They are my people,' and they will say, 'The Lord is our God."

Dear Heavenly Father,

I am so grateful for your provision and your planning! I am thankful that all that I will ever need has been covered by a plan. I am thankful for the gift of an ever-growing faith and relationship with you. Thank you for strengthening me and allowing me to grow to a place where my faith is sturdy in you. I appreciate that when I continually set you before me, that my faith cannot be shaken. Help me to remember all that you are, and all that you can accomplish even through my life. Let me be willing to embrace all that you have given me and your plan, no matter what it looks like, with strength, boldness and confidence.

In Jesus' name, Amen.

Take a moment to listen....what in your own heart do you want to say?

What is He saying back to you?

Philippians 4:6
"Do not be anxious about anything, but in every situation, by prayer and petition, with thanksgiving, present your requests to God."

Dear Lord,

Let me come to you with a prayer of thanks to you. It is a privilege to serve you and to be loved by the one true King of Kings and Lord of Lords. You are the creator of the universe and love me enough to also be my Father, my guide, my provider, my protector, and my best friend. Thank you for allowing me to serve you. You are the one and only God that I can have unshakable confidence in. Knowing that your name is above all names, and nothing is impossible with you. Thank you for loving me enough to be so good to me, even when I least deserve it. I am grateful for all that you are and for not only all that you have done, but all you will do in the future. Let me never take for granted the power of having you in my life or being able to develop a personal relationship with the one who loves me most.

In the name of Jesus I pray, Amen.

Take a moment to listen….what in your own heart do you want to say?

What is He saying back to you?

Luke 11:9
"So I say to you: Ask and it will be given to you; seek and you will find; knock and the door will be opened to you."

Dear God,

I am grateful for all that you have taught me, all that you have opened my heart to see and learn. Thank you for your love, your word, your calling and offering me the ability to have full access to you. Refocus my mind, Lord, keep it focused solely on you and keep my heart open to worship you for all that you are. Help me to continue to seek you first on a daily basis and desire to grow continually in my relationship with you and those you have placed in my life to reach for you.

In Jesus name I pray, Amen.

Take a moment to listen….what in your own heart do you want to say?

What is He saying back to you?

1 Timothy 2:1-4
"I urge, then, first of all, that petitions, prayers, intercession and thanksgiving be made for all people — for kings and all those in authority, that we may live peaceful and quiet lives in all godliness and holiness. This is good, and pleases God our Savior, who wants all people to be saved and to come to a knowledge of the truth."

Dear God,

I am grateful for loving me enough to be willing to sacrifice your one and only son just to have me again! There is nothing greater than that love! Refocus my heart. Let me recognize all you have done in the proper perspective. Encourage my mind to truly be appreciative of the love you have for me each and every day, and let that appreciation motivate me to spread your truth and love to those around me. Let each day be an opportunity for me to do something to grow the kingdom.

In Jesus' name I pray, Amen.

Take a moment to listen....what in your own heart do you want to say?

What is He saying back to you?

Psalm 66:17

"I cried to him with my mouth, and his praise was on my tongue."

Dear Lord,

I appreciate you, from deep within my heart, for your unconditional love for me. I am so grateful that there is nothing that I can ever do to separate myself from your love. I thank you that you love me enough to offer all that you do, not because I could ever have earned it, but simply because you care. Help me to remember what I have learned during this journey. Help me to remember all the things that you have placed in my heart; that the gratitude will not leave my heart when this journey ends, but that it will continue to be in my heart and grow throughout the coming weeks and years. I love you Lord and I thank you for just being you!

In Jesus name, Amen.

Take a moment to listen….what in your own heart do you want to say?

What is He saying back to you?

You made it friend!

I hope that you were blessed by taking this journey and I pray that it gave your prayer life a jump start! It was such a pleasure to create this for you! I look forward to many more ventures together in my upcoming books! I will see you again soon!

~Love and Blessings~

Pastor Rachel

Numbers 6:24-26
"The Lord bless you
and keep you;
the Lord make his face shine on you
and be gracious to you;
the Lord turn his face toward you
and give you peace.

ABOUT THE AUTHOR

Growing up in Virginia, Rachel has had a strong relationship with God from an early age. Through the years, he has led her closer to him and guided her to become a local church minister. During this journey, she created Courtesy Care and Creation Care ministries through her home church. Both of these ministries provided her with an opportunity to reach the community, grow in her faith and follow the nudge of God. After several years of ministering, Rachel answered the call to become a Pastor. Upon answering the call, she created her Rays of Light website, where she provides scriptures, devotions, testimonials and so much more. Rachel's mission is to use her calling to share, encourage, educate, and help others grow in their relationship with God no matter your background. Throughout this journey she has been an excellent example to her three wonderful sons, whom all enjoy diving into the word and showing the love of Jesus to others with her daily. Currently, Rachel serves as Online Pastor at Life Changers Christian Center in Wytheville, VA. When she is not spending time with her boys, leading her local women's ministry, co-hosting Faithful Light Podcast with her dear friend, she is creating new content for Rays of Light. In the future, she hopes to continue to step out into new ventures as God lays them on her heart, and she is excited for the release of future books!

CONTACT THE AUTHOR

Email: Raysoflight.info@gmail.com

Website: https://raysoflightinfo.wixsite.com/raysoflight

Facebook: Rays of Light

Instagram: Raysoflight.info

Please make sure to submit your testimony of blessing and healing you received from this book on the website to make sure it is featured. While visiting the site be sure to subscribe to the website for newsletters, information and upcoming events. Prayer requests are always welcomed and prayed over daily.

Made in the USA
Columbia, SC
23 October 2024

44592596R00041